THE BEAT

SUE ZHU

BFH ACADEMIC PRESS BFH

TITLE: THE BEAT

Author: Sue Zhu
Translators: Wen Xinjiao, Sue Zhu

Publisher: BFH Academic Press
30 Nov, 2022
ISBN: 978-0-473-63323-3

Publishing BFH Academic Press
E-mail
bfhpress@outlook.com

Book Size   6X9 inches

Book Cover Design: Sue Zhu
First Edition November 30, 2022

All rights reserved. No part of this publication may be reproduced, stored in a retrieval system or transmitted, in any form or by any means without prior written permission from the publisher, except for the inclusion of brief quotations in a review.

Sue Zhu, is a New Zealand Chinese poet, artist, promoter of modern international poetry, continental coordinator of the WPM, extraordinary ambassador of Naji Naaman Literature foundation, and Co-founder of the All Souls Poetry. Her poems were translated into over 20 languages, and her paintings can be found on the book cover of worldwide anthologies and were collected by people.

She owns dozens of Chinese and world literary awards, such as the Nosside World Poetry Prize (UNESCO, 2021, 2022), The Naji Naaman literary prize, Best Foreign Writer Award of Premio Internazionale di Poesia I Colori dell'Anima 2022, Best foreign author of Premio 29th Ossi di Seppiadi quest'anno, The Poiesis Award for Excellence in Poetry' in the Rabindranath Tagore Award International, Twice nominated for Pushcart Prize (USA) and interviewed by Publisher Weekly.

She was invited to attend several prestigious poetry festivals such as the 32nd Medellin international poetry festival, The 16th Festival Mundial De Poesia 2022(Venezuela), The 48th Karamanov Poetry Festival 2021 (Macedonia) lll Festival International LA Mujer EN Las Letras (Mexico, by ANHG, UNAM), The V International Meeting of Writers" LA LUNA CON GATILLO" Argentina, The Panorama International Literary Festival (India) in 2020.

TABLE OF CONTENTS

"A BLUE PARADISE AT THE CENTER OF THE SEA" AND FOUR OTHER POEMS — Thoughts on visiting the heart-shaped island of Fiji

MY HEART IS STOLEN 7
TALE 8
YOU WIN MY HEART 9
LISTEN TO EACH OTHER'S HEARTBEAT. 10
LOVE FILLS THE BOOK 11

"THE SEVENTH LUNAR MONTH, WITH SUCH BURNING LOVE" (A Group of Poems) 13

WIND BELL (A Group of Four Poems) 17

ROUND DANCE OF WINE AND COFFEE (A Group of Poems)
A CUE OF SLEEPLESSNESS FROM YOU 19
BLACK COFFEE.. 20
STIR THE COFFEE IN THE TEACUP.............................. 21
THAT IN THE CUP 22
CHARDONNAY WINE... 23
RED WINE SOAKED IN LOVESICKNESS..................... 24

SONATA OF LOVE (A Group of Poems)
EVERY SNOWFLAKE COMES WITH ITS OWN METAPHOR.. 25
SERENDIPITY 26
CLEANSING 27
READ YOUR MESSAGE IN A PLANE........................... 28
THE TWINKLING CANDLE 29

DOOR HANDLE	30
DIAMOND RING	31
THE ANSWERS	32
LOVE ON SUMMER ISLAND	33
FLUTE MELODY	34
A SPECIAL GIFT.	35
CONFESSION .	*36*
AFTER TH NIGHT RAIN	37
SECRETS IN THE CASTLE	38
A GRAIN OF SALT WITH A STORY	39
THAT HIGHT	40
THE REASON	41
SNOW FALLING QUIETLY	42
THROUGH THE PINE WAVE	43
BUTTERFLY COCOON	44
HARVEST WHEAT IN AUTUMN	45
FAREWELL .	46
VIEW OF THE BACK	47
DRINKING FACE TO FACE IN LOVESICKNESS .	48
GIVE YOU A BUNCH OF DRIED ROSES	49
WHEN YOU WITHDRAW FROM RIVERS &LAKES	50
LOVE MESSAGE DELIVERED BY A SWAN GOOSE	51
WAITING FOR THE FULL BLOOM.	52
RAIN, WHERE ARE YOU?	53
LOVE ME, A DIFFERENT FIREWORK	55
DUSK	56
LET YOU BREATHE LOVE DEEPLY AND FREELY	56
PERSONAL VIEW	57
OCEAN FLAMES	58
CRYSTAL WINE GLASS.	59
THE CLIMBING ROSE	60
LAVENDER	61
PEACH FLOWER IN PRE-EXISTENCE	63
MAPLE LEAVES.	64
LOVE WRITTEN IN THE STARS	65

CONCERTO OF LOVE (A Group of Poems)
THE FIGURE BY THE RIVER IN EARLY SPRING.........66
MEMORIAL RITUAL 67
WHILE THE SUN WAS ABOUT TO SET 68
HYDRANGEA 69
TO MY DAUGHTER...70
THE APPLE OF STRIFE. 71

NOSTALGIC CHANTS (A Group of Poems)
THAT CITY OF SCHOLAR TREE FLOWERS 72
HOMESICKNESS 73
WHEN WILL THE BRIGHT MOON LIGHT UP MY WAY HOME.. 74
AN OUTDOOR MOVIE IN AN AUTUMN.. 75
SEE SNOW FALL... 76
TONIGHT.. 77
HOMESICKNESS IGNITED BY FIREFLIES 78
SEEKING EVIDENCE.... 79

WATER VARIATIONS (A Group of 4 poems)
A DROP OF WATER..80
WATER, BUT NOT WATER...81
WATERY LOVE.. 82
WATER WONDER.. 83

"A BLUE PARADISE AT THE CENTER OF THE SEA" AND FOUR OTHER POEMS

— Thoughts on visiting the heart-shaped island of Fiji

MY HEART IS STOLEN

For an area of 29 acres, to me
You are not an island, but a fine peach-shaped pin
On the chest of the sea

Like a jade carpet, with fine foam at arm's length
Your name is chanted by the tide, "Heart-shaped Island"
It's a verb, an adjective, a
Tidal tense for open competition

Bad at swimming but rich in body water, tourists
Come to you in admiration, a distant viewer
Let's fly an aerial camera on wings, from above
Outflanking your foyer

The lofty sentiment of giant waves' claps is deafening
Such surging excites your admiration, touches the string of your love
The bustling sails of worship come and go at will
But you refuse to embrace love

The vulgar and the fickle visit you time and again
They fail to get your pulse and heartbeat
Alone, you only want to live with

the eternal water and the warrior on the wave
The petals enclose time to make, at its bottom, the seeds
Which are deeply rooted at the center of the surfboard
In the blue heaven of ocean, you accept the one only*
Whose name is
The surfer

    * The heart-shaped island in Fiji is a private island that mainly provides accommodation for world-class surfing competitions. Nearby is the most famous wave spot "Cloud break," which is a paradise for surfers.

A TALE

The small island and the sea
Who loves deeper

A glance at the spray, makes the sea, buzz at once
The small island is shy, listening quietly
Dark clouds, hurricanes, and the moody sea
A seagull flying at the sea, steadily

Tells that in 1643, from the garden of heaven
a peach pit fell, into the hands of the sea
Many years later, a ripe fruit
Grew into a green heart-shaped amber

YOU WIN MY HEART

Just let a skiff
Open up that waterway
To reach you

Romantic but lonely, you, in the ocean
Take the roar of the waves, for an oath
Take the flighty of clouds, for romance
You let slip -

How much sincerity traveling over mountains and waters
How much kindness from rosy clouds glittering on the water
How much perseverance of light sails riding on long wind and waves
How much loyalty piled up by the redness of fish's fins

"A heart-shaped petal can only hold one drop of water"
Do you see a Jingwei* bird?
Leave the sky behind
Carry with beak a long oval board full of colourful pebbles and shells
Fly from the faraway Orient

Jingwei bird, a bird in Chinese legend that never gave up holding stones to fill the sea.

LISTEN TO EACH OTHER'S HEARTBEAT

Meet here
Deep in the vast sea

The dull blue feelings are in constant shakes by the sea
Waves leap onto the beach, freely go in and out of your hair
You are in such a calm

In the sound of waves, how many epochs have you been waiting
Flowering seasons, with nobody's attention, have passed in wind and rain for centuries
Your staying with hope — how persistent it is

The sky is high, birds fly in a hurry
The empty wind has no place to stay
Seagrass sways in the doomed fate of life
You know, keeping company is a mere fantasy

Orange love scatters and falls into the early morning and afternoon
Your skirt dances with waves, your hairband flies in air
Your opening shirt has the remaining warmth of autumn
In a rosy dusk, he joyfully arrives

Listen to your heartbeat, and give you
His youthful uneasiness

LOVE FILLS THE BOOK

Head over heels for you? These are words from my heart
Make the feeling into a story
With a blue pen and ink, light green paper and inkstone, and butterfly flower envelope

The romance begins at a planned voyage
Happy spray follows all the way and makes wet
The ship, the mast, my distant gaze
And your lonely and drooping eyelashes

The wind direction is predicable, it travels all the way south
Across the blue sea
Hardly stops at the long journey by white sails

The figure returning to shore anchors in the moonlight
Hanging around is a newly lit bud
However frequently the night chill passes
The flame of desire will neither go out, nor die out

Why seeking overly decorated deliberate description?
A memorable and pure notebook, plain as me
On the title page, it's written, "Heart-shaped Island, first met in 2019"
On the back cover, it's painted "See you again"

How about the solid content? Leave to you to ma

"THE SEVENTH LUNAR MONTH, WITH SUCH A BURNING LOVE" (A Group of 7 Poems)

1.
In a special month, it's destined to have much water
The earth is decorated with many tattoos, it's rain
Stroke by stroke, outlining you in dots
Here clearer, here messier
Wind would neither care, nor inquiry
Just let heart be the guide

2.
The moon is setting, crows are crying, fishermen's lamps are going out
Some people lift cups of wine, savouring it over nice glossy lips
Lighting up the fine moment and beautiful scene. Some other people
Hold the thoughts tight; blend them with wine, for a dose of medicine
To quell the old illness, only to sink from the dark to an abyss
Away from them, countless swaying wishing lights
Slowly swim to the heart of the river, the most dazzling one
Has a heart beating in unison with mine?

3.
The stream flows constantly, over the rock

Moonlight looms, with vague body languages express
gently and genuinely the slimmest   probability in the universe
You hug and massage me
I have indulged myself, only to become smoother
The stream never detours, The rock never budges

4.
Amid two petals
Erects a thick flower
It's a red rose on top
From the relic of many years ago on a Qixi *Festival
By a gardener, with the same surname
The bronze skin, broad palms
Holding and lifting the sunlight
carefully remove its sharp edges with a blade
almost perfect of the body
Specially made for tonight only
Blooming among the lovers' lips

5.
A silent willow stands, like a harp
Notes have long lost, but there are some tones over the strings
Bringing back the memory of
The sadness at the fingertips

The evening wind is gentle
The mountains start the countdown
Of the time to dawn, the birds' chorus
And the wind speed

After flower buds split
One after another, they will all
Step on the seven pedals, pluck the colourful flowing clouds

Some expectation matches the time and scene
It's just that the moon is still a crescent
Shy of a full exposure

6.
We really are
Two destined stars in the Milky Way, gazing afar
In a distance of light years
How can we meet to hug and kiss one another?

After the rain at the Qixi Festival, we make a colorful bridge
To meet, you are still young
I still have beautiful ink-like dark hair
For that word
We are still longing

7.
Not to mention, The faded peach blossom, the passed rain of pear blossom
Not to mention, The absent white dew, the incomplete moon

Just recall the cowherd and the weaver girl
And the sleepless magpie. Just recall
In Heaven and Earth
The flooding Wangchuan River

Willing to accept a virtual plot, And the jackdaw's prophecy
Accept the impermanence of the world
Accept the possible of the impossible

But I have not the least willingness to recall
A name gone with the wind

*Note: The seventh day of the seventh month in the lunar calendar is the Chinese Valentine's Day (Qixi Festival), which this poem is written for.

WIND BELL (A Group of Four Poems)

1.
Always in the dream. Combing
The long and short lines of day
Drawing the curling, spreading and fleeting clouds
Writing the mood of sea water touched by the full moon
Spring flowers and autumn fruits, finally back to the earth
Flying snowflakes, as keepsake of love promise
Until you have kissed my forehead
The sleeping Aurora gets back her heart beating
In the wind, we have loved, walked together
Our stories
Travel afar...

2.
the love inspirator, if you won't come
Myriads of hills and rivers, and floating clouds stay rigid.
If you will come
the secret is revealed to the whole world
Perhaps, I am your most direct beneficiary
Not knowing what is love, simply
in your tender caring
I confide without reservation
Believe me, and listen now...

3.
The wind, attempts to fly over the mountain top
In waiting, days have been squandered
year after year

Lily flowers fill up the road entrances in autumn, one rainfall
comes on the heels of another
I yearn for some confession

Without you, the gold-like sheen will be tarnished
Lilies cannot but hold back their songs, in silence till death
Without me, your covert and caring visits
won't be leaked to the world

We are one another's
carrier of being and expressing
with affections, hanging on a string

4.
Too heavy in longing, too light in words
To dodge gravity, declining abrupt ascending
Leaving only one string of care
angling the blue sky

The promise, disperses in a breath
I fail to hold, the lingering sound
from wafting afar across the mountain

You come, giving me the first cry
You go, leaving me the dirge of living under others' roof
You are the one who tied the bell of my life, and
the only one who can untie it

ROUND DANCE OF WINE AND COFFEE
(A Group of 5 Poems)

A CUE OF SLEEPLESSNESS FROM YOU

At the quiet night, my heart was as calm as water
It was time for a scoop of warm coffee

Too reluctant to say
Because any word would stretch the rainy season
The skirt was washed many times
Hung upside down heavily at the balcony

Turning the clock hands backward
To see cherry blossoms, drizzle, autumn wind, the cold moon
Fragments of your scent wafted through the ancient road and pavilions
Roamed in finely decorated dreams

Got up early next morning
It was not the clear dew that wetted the window
It was not that the bird knocked on the door
It's not the time difference of different regions

It was you last night and me with excessive drinking
Gave each other
Some hints
Again

BLACK COFFEE

The smooth porcelain cup firmly sits in the palm
Thought drop into it, bit by bit

The hotness of the water causes swelling heartache
This is not what you, in your past life
Expected of the current one

Wrong season is doomed to no harvest
You fail to enter a white sugarcane forest

The hand that picked you stirs the foam
Those who know you savour the happiness coming after the suffering

I am one of the later
After autumn
Before the arrival
Of a rain

STIR THE COFFEE IN THE TEACUP

Flat white coffee is an irresistible temptation
The favourite color of green gives way to brown

The bottom of the cup was once clean with floating green
Attracted the calls of nestlings
Rose-shaped spots climbed the side of the cup

The cold evaporated in a downpour
The autumn stole the throne
It's not your fault to desert the city and hide in my teacup

Come here, settle here
Pick out the twilight with a spoon
Allow you to leave some blank
Let me free my endless imagination
In the heart of tea

*Flat white coffee is a kind of coffee that has even white milk foam and is as smooth
as silk.

THAT IN THE CUP

Your existence is to fill the void
Choose to stay at a corner under all eyes
The autumn water in the cup is blended with sweet and bitter

Heart is dazzled by the bright red
Shake gently, drink heavily with the thousand-year sorrow

Marking day and night as clear as the black and white
You and I are in love in our pre-existence
Then meet each other by chance in this life

No need to go into details about
Who triggers the volcano of past happenings?
And whose fingertip touches
The little grass in a vast area

CHARDONNAY WINE

Along the curve of time
From the bottom up to the smooth neck
It seems your world is comprehensible at one glance

No ups and downs at heart
The clearness is stretching out between the brows Upon
looking at your deep silence, words are held back

Fine bubbles gather around the cork
Want to speak with whom? Or
Seal off the in and out of the wind
After a few flicks, they disappear wearily

Lips and teeth are tightly closed
The moment you open your mouth
Words, as I know, make you sad again

Maybe the best is
To keep as tight-lipped as the bottle

Chardonnay is a white wine, clear and transparent. It is
the main composition of sparkling wine and champagne.

RED WINE SOAKED IN LOVESICKNESS

Failing to hold the hand of fate
You jumped off

Once the most beautiful flower on his shoulder
You were examined time and again in the arm of the autumn

Entangled in the vines, a well-kept secret
Was planted before the autumn harvest
A glass of red wine was your nirvana and rebirth

Those who held the cup stopped at fine sipping and drinking
The heartbroken red sobbed
With a longing that was slowly climbing up

SONATA OF LOVE (A group poems)

EVERY SNOWFLAKE COMES WITH ITS OWN METAPHOR

The little one, swaying its feet by my forehead
Must not have been in a dreamland, with cicadas ringing in red cherry trees
Flocks of white butterflies flying and stopping

This untimely and unexpected encounter is beyond me
For several days, hardly have I had the thought of writing
Its figure overlaps with the distant light source

Oh, little white butterflies
With the past noble and affluent life
Fly out of the slender river in this life
Cross the sea with natural mission

For the sky
For the earth
Or just for that one person
With that snow deep in the heart

SERENDIPITY

Under the moonlight, above the flowing water
It is everywhere, and it is nowhere
If such mystery is interpreted as people, things, or situations
The interpretation is pale and good for nothing
Where are you from, for what? You are---

The arrival of the breeze when flowers open
The rain in a blink of an eye when the sky bursts into tears with joy
The hungry traveller lodged at dusk in the smoke of the kitchen chimney
The reincarnation of dandelion seeds at the foot of the snow-capped icy mountains

Wherever you go, you turn things around:
Roaming fish chases one after another
Tender leaves take in sunlight's calcium
Meteorites kiss the earth across light years

You are, A kind existence in fate
The shade of willow planted unintentionally
The togetherness slipped from hands
The blossoms missed by the butterfly flying sideways

You are the thunder rumbling away instantly
The Immortality at the right time
Or an early death at the wrong time

CLEANSING

The autumn breeze starts at dusk, and the heavy rain usurps the role of the host
Getting an umbrella, rose flower fertilizer, rabbit's hay ready
All creatures are going to hibernate

Thin frost and thick fog occupy half of the solar terms
The huge fireball is often hidden
Occasionally burns holes in the clouds

Every star
Every terrace
Every shadow made by whispering lovers at the window
Guides me to identify the golden wing of time

It's a cool but nice autumn with plentiful rain
I don't have to be as stingy as in summer
I don't have to use it prudently, cleanse over and over
Every day inside and outside

White doors and windows, bed sheets, marble countertops
In this season of blooming lilies
We boil rain and snow, drink the sake
In every slightly drunk momentWe love fully each other,
Pure and clean

READ YOUR MESSAGE IN A PLANE

Every lonely word
Like a traveller who trudges a long distance.
When shall we meet at a corner of the world and plant a red bean
Life will be released from suffering at some moment

The airflow in the cabin under pressure inflates the sleeplessness
And takes away the temperature from your body
The black outside the porthole is even boundless

All words are actually redundant
Except for two, rippling in my heart
The weightless pen falls in the sky
It turns out that the person and the city is not far away

Turning on the light, I look at the lines of words
Try to re-organize your text
Delete "worry", erase "lovesickness"
But fail to dodge the shooting star
That shoots down at full speed
The teardrops at the corner of my eyes

THE TWINKLING CANDLE

Burning inch by inch is just to accompany you
To walk through the buildings, streets, jungles
Till deep at night

Steady and calm steps
Cause the panic in my heart
in an instant hesitation
Lies between the narrow light and your closer hair

Thanks to the uncertainty of the dark
We are united as one
crossed arms shield away the wind
And my faint light
Is enough to drive away beasts afraid of light

You don't have to thank me for this journey
Those afraid of darkness have some hesitation
Calling for sparkling eyes
To steady the wobbly steps

My only wish is that
Whoever following in my footsteps
Love you as much as I do
Ready to shed the last drop of tear
Just For you

DOOR HANDLE

Autumn rain is coming, sycamore leaves are falling
Night gets colder, the dream manor gets colder
Silent line drawing starts with speechless
You and I have a warm grip

Your life is clear and cannot be overlooked
But is often ignored
Throughout the years, it keeps the memory of the spring breeze touching the faces
The indelible memory of turning around resolutely and leaving

Zooming in on this stiff world
Memories are diluted in social affairs
Looking outside the door, or staying alone with the red candle
Plain eyes are shining like stars

When all the leaves fall asleep
Time stays outside of life
When the footsteps go from near to far
All the waiting is brought to an abrupt end

Do you still remember
That night
A soft hand has held you gently for a while
To reveal a full moon in the autumn breeze

DIAMOND RING

Upon wearing it on the ring finger, a question pops up
Exposed to the dust of time, will it still be
As clear and flawless as before

It is born with gold in fate, quenched into shape
And designated for a symbolic meaning

Wiping repeatedly becomes a habit
More often, you are the tester
To get the deepest insight

It is like stars, shining and eternal
Or like the morning dew
Left on the edge of a leaf
Vanishing in the heat of the sun

THE ANSWER

Uphill, downhill. Suddenly, you ask
what is love
I'm speechless
Blurt out
At daytime, you watch the sun
At night, please
Just watch the moon

LOVE ON SUMMER ISLAND

Sleeping in the quilt during the day, wandering under the moon in my dream
Under the midnight sun, sipping tea, listening to the sound of flowers' opening, enjoying the leisure time
On this summer island of the "Road to the North"

The long bridge links its time inside and outside
The second clock hand encircles the time one round after another
Beyond the end of the bridge, time becomes meaningless

Salt-like sweet words are bathed in the sea to become water
Love words are plainly said to become the mountains

Day can be loved to become night
Night can be loved to become the day
The length of love can be marked as infinity
The reef after tide can be loved to become
One star

✦ Norway's Summer Island is planned to become the world's first time-free zone

FLUTE MELODY

The seasonal whistle makes the sound again
The skirt with floral corners swings
Fluttering hair like butterflies
with folded wings kept open

The old July gives no surprise
Gardenias, hydrangeas, and humble plantains
Creep out
From the pipe of the flute

The familiar melodic sound
Floats up and down between the sky and the earth
The lovely notes drive away the loneliness
Of the shy footpath

I am not part of the sound that you make
But a few words
Hesitated and stopped between lips
And linked probably to the cloud and wind

A SPECIAL GIFT

I really want to be
That slender clip on your tie
Sticking to your heart
When you feel proud
Unbutton your suit
Everyone can see
The shiny me
No one would
Send another similar one
To you

CONFESSION

The bright moon throws its secrets
Into the sea
One by one

Thus, the seawater
Becomes restless
From then on

AFTER THE NIGHT RAIN

Rolling up the secrets
Flower petals grow inward and tight
To keep out the spring breeze of the city

Wait for the hands
Holding you gently but firmly
To sprinkle a pink rain, just for you

Last night, high wind passed
Early this morning, flowers fell down

If you will come, please
Just lean down and listen to
The shattered lovesickness all over the ground

SECRETS IN THE CASTLE

A city, a little creature, a scripture
Serene and peaceful

An apricot flower follows the path of time
Sends greetings with whiteness twice a year. And I love
The winter one upon the arrival of the heavy snow

If it was not for a few sparrows, chirping
Some light ink was splashed on the branches
Apricot blossom would be just as white, quiet, and flawless
As my understanding of the true nature of the world

Why was there a sound of the horn to break the city?
Shooting a bow into the melancholic cloud caused the rain to be unease
The boundless ashes, since then, grazed in the sky

How I wish I could reincarnate that apricot flower
Let it bloom and wilt
Reach a consensus with time and war
Men are the sky, women are the earth
And it will never be the one in utter isolation

A GRAIN OF SALT WITH A STORY

Born to be loved by the sea
It was willfully swimming

After reading the mermaid story by chance
It had a restless thought
About the lights on the shore, the singing prince

Followed a big tide, swam into a beach pool
Felt the warmth that it had never had before
After that
A kind of compulsion became stronger at each step

One second before closing its eyes
It heard the quarrel over the spoons
A man said it was too salty
A woman said it was too bland

THAT NIGHT

You lay your head on me, I lay mine on grass
Together, we look up at the night sky and recall the past

By the river, the pebbles at your feet
Sing loud to you
The nursery rhymes reverberated by the wind

Mounting a bamboo pole, I pretend to be the groom
Like riding a horse, I run after your floral skirt
The hair braid stops wearily at dusk
Home, right over there

Twist a few strands of chimney smoke into light ink
Mark your eyebrows and eyelashes
Read, from your clear and bright, the scenery

The evening with green willow and red flowers
The early summer with flying wind and butterflies
The neighboring landscapes and rivers
And at this moment, the moonlight over the branches

I will keep this posture, until
The fish in the water settled down to the bottom
The morning glow kisses the lake water
The dew sneaks up our shoes

The sleepless eyes keep focusing on
The book of love proverb keeps opened
They all refused to close

REASON

Rain falls because of cloud
Cloud surges because of wind
Wind rises because of a story
Halfway into the story, the two protagonists
One changes makeup
The other removes makeup
Who first leaked out the message
And handed over the sky

SNOW FALLING QUIETLY

Pile up a scene of dialogue
As if last night's spring breeze suddenly opened a myriad pear blossom

In the fireplace, pine cones ignite loneliness
The flame, in rhythm and cadence
Copies a painting that is bright and dark, cold and warm

Like a wooden fish, the pendulum knocks and waits
Vague lip languages of each another
During the hiatus between cheering-ups
Are full of odd and dead themes

Speechless, face to face
Outside the window, heavy snow are falling
Relentlessly

THROUGH THE PINE WAVES

Long hair, pulled over the right shoulder, revealed your side face
We, as well as the rippling moonlight in the lake
kept too many tacit agreements

Did you still remember? The moment you leaned over,
a wind passed by, the crystal-clear moon was so bright
It shined through the light clouds

How many such moments that we had in a lifetime
would become another eternity
I learned to accept regrets
Kept on running no-stop with lingering thoughts

The only thing that could stop me
was not the booming roses, or the whispering pollen
My darling, please cross the pine woods in the soughing wind
carry the autumn's gifts --- the crisp pine cones, and bring me home

O, my worrying and lonely heart
Hungry for lights

BUTTERFLY COCOON

Floral scent overflows the boudoir
A sigh is hung on the treetop

The world is in silence
Starlight passes through the window lattice paper
One tinder is enough to set the prairie ablaze

The motto of love is still there
Waxed and sealed to avoid the worldly city
By a pair of slender hands

Right now, a cocoon begins to squirm
Only because of
the summer winds

HARVEST WHEAT IN AUTUMN

Because of you, I only care about warm colors
Make them the label of this season

Meeting one another is a promise from a previous life
Not to be missed in this life

The wheat and the blade that is plump, round and sharp
Admire each other
The beginning of owning each other
Is doomed to be the end of one life

If this is our only way of love
Well, don't stop harvesting
Let me fall asleep in your arms
And never awake again

FAREWELL

That night, smiling, staring and turning around
The farewell has been taken away by wind

Saxophone made a gentle narration in the light
Over the years, one should not stand in a sad and
miserable posture

Longing like grass grows to the waist gradually
I keen to go to the orchid pavilion more and more
Read the characters on the pillars and feel the scent left
by you

Between farewell and goodbye
I can only do two things every day:
Breathing and
Missing you

VIEW OF THE BACK

Watched from afar, thousands of miles far
In the frozen memory, snow flew in the north and
covered the fields and mountains

Jet-black hair was inlaid with white snowflakes
Palms were put together to melt the ice cold with strands
of tenderness

On the roofs and treetops, birds shook their wings
Measure the faraway distance in creaky steps

Snowflakes slid into the collar, further down
To the pounding heartbeat
Like cotton candy, snow wrapped the teenager
Layer upon layer, to bury the missed past

The story of youth was pure white
In turning around, it couldn't be kept anymore
The plum blossoms withered one after another
That affectionate melody of "Plum Blossoms in Three
Movements"
was no longer played
by anyone

GIVE YOU A BUNCH OF DRIED ROSES

The loving April
Threads the lively words in the fine rains
Like red chilies hanging under the eaves

Wind notices something quiet and bright
And brings the whispering of one home to another

Here comes the story, spreading across long streets and short alleys

At this moment, the bright sun pours its light
Onto wide green fields, big trees with open chests
And a bunch of roses hanging upside down on the transom window

You are a porcelain
Slim and smooth, shiny and clean
With a long neck and perfect curvature
Holding roses' dried body
To make up the spring scenery for room

Not that being obsessed with a long-lasting beauty
is for a bystander's examining
But rather that they unintentionally bring the best in each other, though short
But in the eyes of an admirer
It is etern

DRINKING FACE TO FACE IN LOVESICKNESS

Tonight, moonlight and wine are both in the glass
Waiting for the wind to stop touching trees

Think of you, thousands of miles away
Like an elusive cloud
Coming or not, always lingering on my mind

Solidify the moment into a full moon
Let myself bloom like sweet osmanthus
Just in case you come along the dusty roads
You will not lose your way

The overflowing lovesickness dyes the densely woven
warp and weft of the heart
Raise your glass, drink with me
Look into my clear and bight eyes, watch the mist and
rain in the wine bottle

Don't ask the blue sky why time flies
While being drunk, express fully
Our love and affection
Just like the full moon high in the sky

WHEN YOU WITHDRAW FROM RIVERS AND LAKES

At the green willow bank, I dry up the saltiness and bitterness for you
Hold the wind with the palms' warmth
Keep off wet cuffs

With weary steps and eyes
You look for routes in a changed world
And the eyes will be instantly recognized

Holding hands with footpaths to recall the joy of yesterday
Watching floating clouds to feel happy about spring thunder and autumn rain

You need no more words, so do I
Let time bypass home. At the water's end
Turn south

The silhouettes of the same frequency overlap in the sunset
A gardenia
Opens in the dreams of the remaining years

LOVE MESSAGE DELIVERED BY A SWAN GOOSE

At that time, the smoke of the wind and the chimney
Were soft and carefree
New petals of roses grew in the love note
Just looked at the twinkling stars if it did not come

Worried about the wild goose who fell out and lost the messages
Worried about the cyclist who forgot to open the green door
So put the letters on the counter of the post office
Stack after stack, flat and neat

Sent out budded roses
Received flying snow like goose feathers
Seeds fell between the lines
Flowers bloom in the next spring

Colourful clouds in the sky lingered affectionately
Magpies in the forest brought romantic news
Hovering just for one person, for a lifetime
The door latch at night was moved only for him

WAITING FOR THE FULL BLOOM

Sleepless thought is still awake in the deep night
Like a firefly carrying a lamp
Flying different routes to decipher
Light smiles at night

Listen to the trickling sound of water
It glides over the slope and slowly goes down along grooves
And finally merges with the sea
To make a salty cruising dreamland for fishes and seaweeds

Faded pyjamas of flowers are loose and baggy
Songs of insects are kept in the past
Some love and kindness wrap around the hibernation bed
In the soft and even breathing, soothing the cold night

Right now, if one can walk through deep jungles
Cross the less travelled mountain trails
Pass through the light rain under the street lamp
Connect the rainbow dreams one after another

Are they all waiting
For the arrival of the full bloom

RAIN, WHERE ARE YOU?

Wondering where is the rain
The water level of the reservoir cannot stop decreasing
The alarm of life is sounding. I know
This year, I cannot neglect a drop of water

More and more things get dusty
Cars, windows, and roof sinks
I can tell myself to turn a blind eye to them
But my unease just grows day by day

Fine cracks gradually appear in the glass-fibre swimming pool
The illusion of time flows in the circulation of water
Odd pieces of sludge gather at the bottom of the pool
Green moss skillfully grows along its sidewalls

Rain, rain, rain --- I pray
these days, in the quiet night
The hearty rain seems to get my prayer, at daybreak
Pours down torrentially

The rainbow is reflected in the blue water of the pool
White clouds fall into the green manor
Everything that catches the eye is comfortable, beautiful

Refreshing and clear

Cannot let go for a long time
The worries confined in the heart. Guilty and struggling--
Are they also hungry for a rain of soul?
In this winter, it fills up our sea of hearts

LOVE ME, A DIFFERENT FIREWORK

The love of a firework is enough
To ignite the mood of night
In an instant, thousands of dazzling spots
Drive away loneliness

No need to deliberately search in the dark
The charming peacock
Opening feathers again and again
Vying for attention of many a pair of eyes
That are looking up and above

Fascinating, dazzling, shooting high and far
The fragrance of the night blooms
Can hardly conceal
The bursts of strong smell of burning feathers

Fortunately, I have similar attributes to them
Except that my love
Need no looking up or sigh

Inside our house, a different firework
A steady dining table, firewood, rice, oil and pepper salt
Not dazzling, not hasty
At all

DUSK

With no intention to dodge the day, the moon
Pauses between the tops of two Manuka trees

In the blink of an eye, the tide pours in
The long oars of the rubber dinghy cut open the silk water surface
Kingfishers wake up joyfully and sing loudly

Busy women in the garden
And clovers with dew
Are in the giant shadows cast from east to west
Now, all those people feel
The chill in the autumn air

The sunlight travels sluggishly over the roof
Onto their backs, shoulders and feet, and before their eyes
Everything becomes clear

The sunlight travels sluggishly over the roof
Onto my back, shoulders and feet, and before my eyes
Everything becomes clear

The dew is a diamond, the sea a mirror
The sky an inverted ocean
The earth is a wooden boat, carrying me
Into the rosy dusk

LET YOU BREATHE LOVE DEEPLY AND FREELY

The way you are asleep
How shall I love you

Let me be the sunshine, allows you running tirelessly
But I worry that rain and wind would come at deep night
Before I reach you, you already caught a cold

Let me be the tide, wandering with you
But I worry that the wind would break the blue waves
Before the arrival of the ark, you would fall into the bottom of the sea

Let me be the stream, moistening your arduous journey
But I worry that the tributary could not break into the desert
Your chapped lips could not say, you love me

Let me start to write about love affairs and worldly affairs
But I worry that the tinder on paper would not start
The chimney smoke in the world
You would be too weak to blow away the dust

Let me just be the fresh air, surrounding you
In nose and mouth, in the heart
Let you breathe love deeply and freely

PERSONAL VIEW

Earthling up, germinating, and pruning, then attracting butterflies
Today, it is he who buries the flowers
How grateful do roses feel

From birth to death in reincarnation
Never left the embrace of one person

Treat him as parents or lover, or even as God
But not as a gardener
holding scissors
In the garden

OCEAN FLAMES

The fate of my pre-existence
Must have been tied to them

The two feuding antagonists
Across the freezing and boiling points
Are sketched many times by preference
And pulled into the canvas of emotions

Traveling in the long river of time, glamour and decline
Evenly divide downstream from turbulent waves
After the hustle and bustle stops, the gentle and full warmth
In the clear sky, will make the world green in the wind

Looking back in the blinking lights under the stars
I was once the insect flying and dancing over flames
And once the smallest sperm whale
Amid giant blue waves

CRYSTAL WINE GLASS

After a long journey of delivery, my dear
Please receive it

The fine sands of time fall through the worldly net
The blue crystal in the palm has a hint of cloud
Encircling yesterday's silence and confusion

The fire dragon wanders around inside the body
No alcohol is needed for combustion. The empty cup
upside down, is drunken for memory

It is fragile. You must remember to
Hold it gently
Handle it carefully

LAVENDER

When you start to wear elegant purple dresses
The front door of your boudoir cannot stand the endless
knocking
I will not follow the crowd
But on sunny days, close eyes and think of you

Those fabulous wings
Dressed in fine but greedy attire
Fly into your fragrance, get addicted to
your shallow dimples

Some names must be your taboos
Such as gardeners, lovers, or strangers carrying baskets
and scissors
They use you as a metaphor
To interpret their selfish love by way of destruction

Neither do I want to disturb your flowering period
Nor utter all my compliments
I wait for the wind to bring in white silk brocade, a
crystal bottle, and even a strand of gold thread
To keep your essence

In dreams, I take care of you for you to grow
And use a drop of tear
To heal the wound of night

THE CLIMBING ROSE

The seed that sprout and bloom by the window
Should come from another world

Leave it alone, let it go
Growing wantonly, step by step out of sight

Finally, I have to look up
To see its corolla piercing the sky

The southern hemisphere in June is in winter with
frequent rain and wind
Hardly has the rose learned how to keep its fragrance
from the wind and rain
It fades and withers

I have treasured a bottle of its essential oil
But been reluctant to take out the oil early to make up for
The days without it

PEACH FLOWER IN PRE-EXISTENCE

Upon arrival at a river
The tide of heart
Should skip the meeting with the moon

In the red and green of April, you have been here
After traveling downwind along a 180-mile waterway

By the river banks there are winding ridges of fields,
flying butterflies
And rape plants in full bloom

Punting with a pole, beating clothes for washing
To the rhythm of spring breeze

On that wooden suspension bridge, one can see
Dainty fingers are picking up
A green and fresh tea leave, in the whistling of the
willow leaves

I have actually not been to the Qiupu River
It is from the many waves left on paper
I imagine it

I even believe that
There was once a peach flower falling from the bank into
the water
Its light pink skirt
Was lifted easily by wind

MAPLE LEAVES

You spend a lifetime
Chasing the trail of the rainbow
With a child's heart
You exude youthful green
When oranges yellow
You produce revelations

Swaying flames
Kindle the fading dusk
Thick snowflakes drift down as a mantle
Turn you into mud

On that sunny afternoon
An unknown elegant youngster
Picked up a piece of the twilight
Rewrote your recurring fate

Bright red is beautiful for its unfailing hue
Mutual sights resume
The whispering of love
Should you thank the young lad
For perpetuating your beauty
Or should he thank you for being his bold mark

LOVE WRITTEN IN THE STARS

When the red apple was handed over, sadness
Intertwined over the barbed wire, at that moment
His only loved one, is nobody but her
A stranger

The youthful restraint quickly passed
They buried the core of the apple in the soil
He said, the bright blooming was like her keep smiling
She said, she was the tree of flowers bearing children for him

Before arrival of the autumn, said goodbye
To each other, two of them
Across time and space, searching for decades

In the spring of 1942, the fruit tree stopped growing
Finally, one day, it was said
Its branches were full of fruits

Notes: This is a true story that happened in a Nazi concentration camp. The moment the kind girl handed out the apple, the two hearts beat as one in adversity and beyond. After the war, they remained single and looked for each other eagerly all over the world. After decades, the lovers finally became a couple.

CONCERTO OF LOVE (A Group of pems)

THE FIGURE BY THE RIVER IN EARLY SPRING

On a bright day
Motor is running, clothes are spinning together

Untangled to air
They happily wait for the sun and wind
To dry and iron them

Nowadays few people
Are willing to repeat the labour of hand washing them
It reminds me of a lady
By the river in early spring

She squatted by the broken ice, washing old clothes
Her slender figure was washed by water again and again
Her swollen hands taking me home are
Half cold
Half warm

MEMORIAL RITUAL

When father was away
I was on the seashore in the southern hemisphere
He banned the news and chose sea as his final home

Every year on death day, my sister goes to the beach
Scatters flower petals one by one, and let them carried away by waves
She always gently says these few words:
I'm here to see you, also on my sister's behalf

All other words are buried in heart
She is afraid, upon saying one more word
The sea waves
Will pour out of her eyes

WHILE THE SUN WAS ABOUT TO SET

While a cat dozed off on the roof
The sun rolled down from its shoulder
To the feet

It stretched and kicked
Opened mouth with sharp little white teeth, "meow meow~"
Headed straight home

The cooking smoke came first, waving at it
The burnt smell of fried fish made its nose running

In the kitchen, mother rolled up her hair bun
With white butterfly-shaped ornaments flying sideways
and spinning in a little tune

It was dusk, in this quiet and cozy autumn
Suddenly, I felt an urge to untie
Her youth-deprived white hair
And let it fly in the wind right before the sunset

Putting a pure wool shawl on her
I would go with her to watch the countless evening lights...

HYDRANGEA

They hold together, enjoy common time, and evenly
share the spring sunlight
They are visited by light wings, who are wondering
which one
Has honey to feed offspring

My late father loved them so much
He fertilized and watered them, talking to himself
frequently:
They are too fragrant to wither
To fly away with the wind

I was the last one to bloom
But eagerly jumped out of the wall
Settled in a foreign land, planted the seeds
In my own garden

Now imitating my father
I dare not to neglect
Each petal
That seems familiar

In the eyes of the gardener
Which hydrangea is indispensable? I don't know
I only found myself to become more and more
Hesitant
Like a bee or butterfly
Like my dad

TO MY DAUGHTER

In the afternoon, I write a long letter, send it with a gift
To you, a sixteen-year-old, in a faraway land

A select group of apples of all time
With the places of origin, marked out one by one

One from the remote Eastern Eden
One golden apple, in the wedding banquet, setting the gunpowder on fire
One passed by the old woman into the window of the Seven Dwarfs' house
One ever appearing in Socrates's class, as a fake
One in Vroom's expectancy theory to be picked only after a hard jump
One dropped by a careless Charles just to awaken the ruminating Newton
One ever crossing the enormous Sahara Desert
One grown on the tree outside the hedge in 1942, as a token of love
One more, from the garden we have cultivated together

These apples, with spontaneous aroma
Make into jam, peerless

Befriending the independent you, for life
In a happy journey

THE APPLE OF STRIFE

Following the doctor's advice, my lover
I'll give you some fresh apples

Go to Scarborough Fair to pick some
Naturally matured, red and green one
Put green ones aside, for now, enjoy red ones early
Whichever are in between, the date of tasting is up to
you to decide

Overly sweet ,　the golden ones①
I would deliberately pass on, because their temptation
Will overwhelm our resistance
Far beyond our lives

①In the legend a golden apple thrown by the goddess of Discord triggered the Trojan War.

NOSTALGIC CHANTS (A Group of poems)

THAT CITY OF SCHOLAR TREE FLOWERS

On the night of the full moon, upon catching a high tide
Those who listen to the wind by the sea
Get a relapse of the old illness

Turning a deaf ear to the sound of sea waves, I draw a pen
Write the white of scholar tree flowers in spring
The one who likes gentle sniff, where are you now

It is said, time will make parted people forget each other
What is not said, it's a bitter medicine
With no guarantee of cure

In the light of a lonely lamp
Somehow, I am sad, because
The place without you
Has now become my hometown

HOMESICKNESS

Here, clouds are bountiful
Wandering in a foreign land

Every time looking up, I cannot but
Wondering
Which one is me?

WHEN WILL THE BRIGHT MOON LIGHT UP MY WAY HOME?

High up in the sky, the round moon
Is not mine, the distance and time
I fail to work out

In the same mood, sleepless as me
Tonight
Choose to look up

With the falling moon in the water
By hands, the yearning
Can be lifted scoop by scoop
And its flowing direction is
Always from south to north

AN OUTDOOR MOVIE IN AN AUTUMN NIGHT

The distant mountain, lying on its side, was drowsy
Naughty stars pulled open the buttons of its nightdress
Exposing its waving silhouette fully

Dispatched by wind into the lake, willow leaves
Detoured to the reeds that are bowing to drink
Stretching out the silk at their fingertips to wipe the moon in the mirror of water

A cricket broke into the garden
Covered with pollen dropped by bees
With red and swollen eyelids, thrusting its slender hind legs
Seeking doctors here and there

Two or three drinking people gathered at a corner
In tipsy dance steps, with rapture
Sighed at the short-lived summer

The street light at the alley was eagerly attentive, throwing its long skirt into the dark
The children after the movie grabbed it, in a flash
Hit the road home

The glittering moonlight tonight suited a mood
With fragments glued together to replay in a dream
A title would appear before dawn
The end

SEE SNOW FALL

One afternoon
The summer wind floods in

No way to decline
Random heat waves sweep past
Perfect for dozing off

In my hometown
The first heavy snow is falling

Cirrus clouds
Are drifting from the north

TONIGHT

Empty all glass bottles with coins
Buy a good night

The faces in the sea are round and simple
Repeatedly raising and lowering heads, and staring
blankly all night

One day, two days, and three days from now, it will be
Frost's Descent day in the lunar calendar
You will be polished sharp and bright

I start to worry about
Those plants that never stop growing
And those people that have lofty hearts

HOMESICKNESS IGNITED BY FIREFLIES

I tripped over a night
With stars smashed by time
Fishing boats on the other side of the river stopped navigation
By lowering their sails
I was once deeply lost in a dream
Along the yellow brick road, I chased a sika deer
Like pear blossom, heavy snow rustled and scattered
Then plunged into the peach flower pool, a thousand feet deep

The sound of idling airplane engines drifted through the hills
The broken wings of the airplane were still trying
To lift air and carry clouds, in order to give birth
To a timely rainfall deeply yearned for by the earth

Who will awake in the season of flooding rivers
And become extremely sad in the life cycle of the dead leaves
Fireflies with lights dash towards the window
I no longer hesitate over a long journey beyond the dream

Now the moon is thin and lean
Full of fragrance of the sweet Osmanthus
Hobbling along the meandering path
A child, whose clothes are soaked by tears
Goes relentlessly to the north

SEEKING EVIDENCE

It is the autumn season
At the thought of the south, the heart beats faster

Where will the passed clouds go?
Those that still stay stubbornly in the garden
Ask the fallen leaves which are visiting here one after another

This city is thought as liveable
With a variety of different accents

A word in an abstruse and obscure slang
Never need a note

Skylarks contend for singing at this moment
The wind is swayed to become disorder
Wild geese fly in a V shape against the current
And pass over in a hurry

Wandering wings
Where will you go
If they are asked aloud
Will they shout out the answer in excitement?

WATER VARIATIONS (A Group of 4 Poems)

The highest goodness is like water. It benefits all things and does not compete. It stays in the lowly places which others despise. Therefore, it is near The Eternal.
------Laozi

A DROP OF WATER

Together be the cloud
Independent be the raindrop

Traveling to ponds, rivers, the vast sea
feed the plant, crops, and the land

Sacrifice yourself be a little ink
Recording a single word of history

See the white sail, you carrying a boat
See the sharp rock, dripping to penetrate stone
See the air out of kettle, the world turns gentle
see all things flourish blooming, you keep silent all time

You are in anywhere, in any shape
to feed our body and our soul
no one would miss out
All your goodness benefit

Who are you
a drop of water

WATER, BUT NOT WATER

No need to award me a crown
People without a sense of crisis
Praise me like beautiful chaos
Give me such nicknames:
Magical fog gathering clouds,
silent drops in the spring breeze,
timely snow promises a good year,
or the ice cube
with clear jade bones

But, really, I am
just a bitter tear, shed from heaven
For kissing the thirsty lip of Gaia
To touch your lost soul

WATERY LOVE

May the tide only bring the love in
for lonely rock, a miracle
soft dreams afterward

May the wave only sway the boat
for the traveller, a destination
shortened to no distance

May the tears flow
for lovesickness, a tale
extend to life's end

May it make anything possible
to be eternal, but nevertheless
Try not to cry much
not to waste it

WATER WONDER

Women are made of water
The saying in a DREAM OF RED MANSIONS

Which drop of water am I?
From the sky to the boundless sea

I'm afraid to accept your love
in zero degrees
or in one hundred degrees

(English translation: Sue Zhu)

THANK YOU FOR YOUR TIME.

Follow Sue Zhu
For exerpts and updates.

Faceook: https://www.facebook.com/sue.zhu.319
Contact Email: windowanswers@live.com

www.ingramcontent.com/pod-product-compliance
Lightning Source LLC
Chambersburg PA
CBHW051700090426
42736CB00013B/2469